Me
and
Systems

JAMES ALLEN TITLES

———○◆○———

Above Life's Turmoil

All These Things Added

As a Man Thinketh

Byways of Blessedness

Eight Pillars of Prosperity

Foundation Stones to Happiness and Success

From Passion to Peace

From Poverty to Power

James Allen's Book of Meditations for Every Day in the Year

Light on Life's Difficulties

Man: King of Mind, Body, and Circumstance

Men and Systems

Morning and Evening Thoughts

Out from the Heart

Poems of Peace

The Life Triumphant

The Mastery of Destiny

The Shining Gateway

Through the Gate of Good

Men
and
Systems

James Allen

Published 2019 by Gildan Media LLC
aka G&D Media
www.GandDmedia.com

Design by Meghan Day Healey of Story Horse, LLC

Library of Congress Cataloging-in-Publication Data is available upon request

ISBN: 978-1-7225-0239-3

10   9   8   7   6   5   4   3   2   1

Contents

Introduction.................................7

Their Correlations and
Combined Results 15

Work, Wages and
Well-Being 27

The Survival of the Fittest
as a Divine Law......................... 37

Justice in Evil 47

Justice and Love....................... 57

Self-Protection: Animal,
Human and Divine..................... 61

Aviation and the
New Consciousness.....................71

The New Courage 79

James Allen: A Memoir
by Lily L. Allen............................ 89

About the Author........................ 97

Introduction

The unceasing change, the insecurity and the mystery of life make it necessary to find some basis of certainty on which to rest if happiness and peace of mind are to be maintained. All science, philosophy, and religion are so many efforts in search of this permanent basis; all interpretations of the universe, whether from the material or spiritual side, are so many attempts to formulate some unifying principle or principles by which to reconcile the fluctuations and contradictions of life.

It has been said that mathematics is the only exact science; that is, the only science that eternally works out true without a single exception. Yet mathematics is but the body of which ethics is the spirit. There is not a mathematical problem but has its ethical counterpart, and the spirit of ethics is as eternally exact as the form of mathematics.

It is being discovered that all natural sciences are fundamentally mathematical. Even music—popularly considered to be as far removed from mathematics as possible—is now known to be strictly mathematical. The science of harmony revealed certain fixed tones which never vary in their relative proportions, and all of which can be numerically resolved. These tones, like the numbers which represent them, are eternally fixed, and though their combinations—also like the combinations of numbers—are infinite, a given combination will always produce the same result.

This mathematical foundation in all things is the keystone in the temple of science, and when sciences are perfected they will be found to be in strict accordance with mathematical laws.

In religion also there are this same mathematical certainty and exactitude, and this mathematical certainty constitutes the "rock of ages," and the "great peace," on which and in which the saints and sages have ever found rest from the stress and turmoil of life.

Human life and evolution at present is the learning of those preliminary lessons which are leading the race toward the mastery and understanding of this basic or divine knowledge; for without such a permanent, exact, mathematical basis, no lesson could be learned. When human beings are spoken of as learning the lessons of God or of life, two things are inferred, namely—(1) a state of ignorance on the part of the learner, and (2) that there is some definite knowledge which he has to acquire. This is seen plainly in a child at school. Its lessons imply that there is a permanent principle of knowledge toward which it is progressing. Without such knowledge there could be no lessons.

Thus when one speaks of erring men as learning the lessons of life, he infers, whether he realizes it or not, the existence of a permanent basis of knowledge toward the possession of which all men are moving.

This basic principle, a knowledge of which the whole race will ultimately acquire, is best represented by the term *Divine Justice.* Human justice differs with every man according to his own light or darkness, but there can be no variation in that Divine Justice by which the universe is eternally sustained. Divine Justice is spiritual mathematics. As with figures and objects, whether simple or complex, there is a right and unvarying result, and no amount of ignorance or deliberate falsification can ever make it otherwise, so with every combination of thoughts or deeds, whether good or bad, there is an unvarying and inevitable consequence which nothing can avert.

If this were not so; if we could have effect without cause, or consequence unrelated to act, experience could never lead to knowledge, there would be no foundation of security, and no lessons could be learned.

Thus every effect has a cause, and cause and effect are in such intimate relationship as to leave no room for injustice to creep in. Nevertheless, there is ignorance, and, through ignorance, the doing of life's lessons wrongly, and this doing of life's sums wrongly is that error, or sin, which is the source of man's sufferings. How often the child at school weeps because it cannot do its sums correctly! and older children in the school of life do the same thing when the sum of their actions has worked out in the form of suffering instead of happiness.

The ground of certainty, then, on which we can securely rest amid all the incidents of life, is *the mathematical exactitude of the moral law.* The moral order of the universe is not, cannot, be disproportionate, for if it were, the universe would fall to pieces. If a brick house cannot stand unless it be built in accordance with certain geometrical proportions, how could a vast universe, with all its infinite complexities of form and motion, proceed in unbroken majesty from age to age unless guided by unerring and infallible justice?

All the physical laws with which men are acquainted never vary in their operations. Given the same cause, there will always be the same effect. All the spiritual laws with which men are acquainted have, and must have, the same infallibility in their operations. Given the same thought or deed in a like circumstance, and the result will always be the same. Without this fundamental ethical justice there could be no human society, for it is the just reactions of the deeds of individuals which prevent society from tottering to its fall.

It thus follows that the inequalities of life, as regards the distribution of happiness and suffering, are the outworking of moral forces operating along lines of flawless accuracy. This flawless accuracy, this perfect law, is the one great fundamental certainty in life, the finding of which insures a man's perfection, makes him wise and enlightened, and fills him with rejoicing and peace.

Take away a belief in this certainty from a man's consciousness, and he is adrift on a self-created ocean of chance, without rudder, chart, or compass. He has no ground on which to build a character or life, no incentive for noble deeds, no center for moral action; he has no island of peace and no harbor of refuge. Even the crudest idea of God as of a great man whose mind is perfect, who cannot err, and who has "no variableness nor shadow of turning," is a popular expression of a belief in this basic principle of Divine Justice.

According to this principle there is neither favor nor chance, but unerring and unchangeable right. Thus all the sufferings of men are right *as effects*, their causes being the mistakes of ignorance; but as effects they will pass away. Man cannot suffer for something which he has never done, or never left undone, for this would be an effect without a cause.

Man suffers through and of himself. Where the effect is there is the cause. Its seat is within, not without. The things which men are reaping to-day are of the same kind which they formerly sowed. The good man of to-day may be reaping the results of past evil; the bad man of to-day may be reaping the results of past good. Seen thus, this divine principle throws an illuminating light on those cases (common enough) where the good suffer and fail, and the bad enjoy and prosper. Things as they are did not spring into existence without a cause. They have behind them a long train of causes and effects, and another such train will follow them in the future. In viewing the objects in a landscape we allow for perspective; we must do the same in viewing events.

This principle of Divine Justice is not distinct from Divine Law. It is the same. Partial men separate justice from love, and even regard them as antagonistic, but in the divine life they blend into one.

Nothing can transcend right. Nothing can be more loving than that we should experience the consequences of ignorance and error, and so become "perfected through suffering." In this Divine Love, which never alters, never errs, never passes over a single deed, we have a sure rock of salvation, for that which could shift and change could afford no foothold. Only in the unchangeable, the eternally true, is there permanent peace and safety. Resorting to this divine principle, abandoning all evil, and clinging to good, we come to a knowledge and realization of that basis of certainty on which we can firmly stand through all life's changes; we have found the rock of ages and the refuge of the saints.

—James Allen
Bryngoleu,
Ilfracombe, England

Their Correlations and Combined Results

There is today a widespread revolt against those modes of human activity designated "Systems," and these systems are almost invariably referred to as something distinct from, and yet directing, controlling or tyrannizing over humanity itself. Thus, the leaders in the revolt referred to, speak of the "commercial system," the "social system," the "competitive system," the "political system," and so on; and the particular system condemned is made responsible for—made the cause of—certain widespread evils, such as poverty, vice, etc., as though "systems" were some sort of discarnate and gigantic despots, enslaving and crushing an innocent and unwilling humanity.

Such an arbitrary and external form of system has no existence; it is a delusion. Human systems cannot be separated from human desires and needs; they are, indeed, the visible outworking of those desires and needs. A system is none other than the combined and concerted mode of action of the community; it signifies a tacit agreement on the part of all, or nearly all, that things should be thus and so; it is a method in which human kind *agree to act*; and as men act, so systems appear, as they cease to act, so they disappear.

And let it be understood that such *agreement to act* has no reference to, or bearing upon, a man's attitude toward a system—whether for or against—but depends upon his actions. A man may violently condemn a system with his lips, yet show that he is in agreement with it in his heart by the fact that he continues to act in accordance with it, to follow it out in his daily life. We are all aware of that form of religious hypocrisy (nearly always unconscious) that continues to commit the sin which it violently denounces; thus showing, in practice, a fundamental agreement with that which, superficially and in theory, is opposed; and this form of unconscious inconsistency is not Confined to religion, it is a pronounced factor in all moral activities, and is nowhere more strongly in evidence than in those directions where the reform of "existing systems" is, theoretically at any rate, the primary aim. Thus, when I had asked some socialists, who condemn the present capitalist system as a system of getting rich on the labor of the poor, why they themselves live on dividends—that is, on the fruits of other men's labor—thus propagating every day that which they denounce as an evil—the reply almost invariably has been, "You should blame the system, not me." This reply shows that such people regard themselves as the helpless victims of a tyrannical something which exists external to, and independent of, themselves and their actions, and which they call a "system." But a little reflection will show that that which they denounce as the "system" is none other than the viewing as evil certain actions *in others* which they regard as good *in themselves*.

Such people being, by their concerted action with others, in agreement with the thing which they denounce, are not merely *accessories* to the "system" which they regard as evil, *they are themselves that system*, and doubtless to many a rampant denouncer of the slayer of the wage-earning lambs might justly be brought the charge—"Thou art the man!"

Human systems are human modes of action which are dependent for their continuance on a fundamental tacit agreement among men to continue to act in the same way; and such agreement implies that those who continue to enact any particular system must be prepared to meet and to accept its disadvantages, as well as its advantages; for in the struggle for advantage there must always be the corresponding disadvantage; in the battle of human interests there must always be both victory and defeat.

Viewed in this light, the term "innocent victims of the system," so much in vogue, is seen to be shallow and delusive. There are no innocent victims of a system in which *all* engage either in the letter or the spirit; if guilt there be, then all are guilty, and the innocence is superficial and apparent, not fundamental and real. In reality, however, there is neither innocence nor guilt attached to a human system which has evolved through long processes of struggle and time. There is merely the victory and happiness on the one hand, and the defeat and misery on the other; and the defeated are not the innocent, nor the victorious the guilty, for both these conditions in social life are the just effects of men's actions, as victory and defeat attach to a battle or a race. To make this more plain, let us take a simple illustration. Here are ten men who mutually agree to engage, among themselves, in certain forms of gambling. Now, the object of each of these men is to win, and so increase his wealth, yet they all know that there is also the possibility of losing; know, indeed, that some must lose, for such is the unavoidable hazard of the game. Immediately these men commence to act by laying down their stakes, they have created a system which might be called "the gambling system," and the advantages and disadvantages of such a system soon become apparent. There is ceaseless fluctuation of their combined wealth—some winning and becoming rich, and then again losing and becoming poor; but ultimately some lose all they possess and have to retire defeated, while others acquire the loser's part and become rich on their gains.

Now, it cannot be said of the winners that they are guilty of exploiting and crushing down the losers; nor can it be said of the losers that they are the innocent victims of the system of gambling in which they are engaged. In the mental attitude and actions of these ten men there is neither innocence nor guilt, but a mutual engagement in a method, with its inevitable results, namely, the reaping of its advantages on the one hand, the suffering from its disadvantages on the other.

In like manner, of the various systems in which men have involved themselves, there are no innocent victims, no guilty tyrants. Victims there are, if men choose to apply that term to the defeated, or to those who, for the time being, are suffering loss, but they are the victims of their own deeds, and not of an overruling and compelling injustice outside themselves. Of the ten men who engage in gambling, none are victimized, none can possibly be victimized, but themselves. Those outside the system—that is, those who do not encourage and propagate it by their acts—remain untouched, uninjured by it. So if our present commercial system should be a "system of greed," as many social reformers style it, then not by any possibility whatever could any but the greedy be injured by it.

Doubtless there is much greed in the world, for in its present stage of evolution, humanity is learning its lessons largely along selfish paths; but greed can never have any existence in an external "system," it can only exist in human hearts, nor can greed injure any but the greedy. Commercialism is free from greed in the hands of those who have destroyed greed in themselves. But they who are greedy will taint everything—even religion—with their own impure condition.

Industrialism, the outworking of a nation's energies and abilities, is wholesome and noble; it is covetousness which produces woe, and the sole sufferers from covetousness are the covetous themselves.

I will here anticipate the common query—"What of the innocent victims of the rapacious company promoter?"—by replying (and this reply will be found adaptable to all human conditions and systems), they are not innocent, but have the same attitude of mind as the unscrupulous company promoter—namely, the desire to obtain money, and as much of it as possible, without laboring for it. The company promoter is the instrument through whom they reap the results of their own greed, and fall victims to their own covetousness.

Social reformers may denounce the system of "capitalism" or "commercialism," but so long as they themselves continue to enact that side of commercialism which is most akin to covetousness, namely, its speculative as distinguished from its industrial side, by keeping a keen eye to "good investments," and following up increased "dividends" with avidity, just so long will that which they call "a system of greed" (and indeed to them it is such) continue.

Those who are striving to live by speculation, on the fruits of another's labors, or who have the spirit so to do should the opportunity arise (and the number of those who are anxious to acquire money without giving its equivalent is very large), should not bemoan the existence of want and poverty, but should perceive and receive such conditions as the inevitable disadvantages of the method which they are acting out, as luxury and riches are its advantages.

The hope of one day becoming suddenly rich without working for it, and living ever after a life of unbroken ease, is a common chimera among the poor. While covetousness continues to sway the human mind, want and poverty will continue.

Men desire, and then they act, and their combined acts constitute what men call "systems." The ten gamblers desired to increase their wealth without laboring for it, and at each other's loss, and they acted accordingly. Their combined actions constituted the system with its combination of results. Systems are, therefore, deeds, the deeds, combined and reciprocal, of a number of individuals; and the so-called evils in the world which men attribute to systems as distinguished from men, are the reactions upon individuals of their own deeds.

A system cannot be "unjust," because men inevitably reap the just effects of their own deeds.

The evils which prevail in the world are indications of justice, not injustice. Poverty and want are the natural disadvantages of the present social life, or system—that is, of the way in which men agree to act. There is suffering, but there is no injustice. It could not be said of those among the ten gamblers who were reduced to poverty, that they were treated unjustly by the winners, or that they were the innocent victims of the system of gambling. Their lot was just; their poverty being the inevitable result of their own actions.

Recently a socialist friend of mine was somewhat violently condemning landlords and landlordism, and I pulled him up by saying—"But why do you condemn landlords, seeing that you are one yourself; have you not, only a few weeks ago, added another piece of land to that which you already possessed?" He replied—"It's the system, not me. So long as the present system lasts I shall have to work with it; but, when it is altered, I shall be willing to give up my land."

If a gambler were continually condemning the "system" of gambling as a bad one, and yet continued to gamble, we should justly say that he was confused both in his morals and perceptions; and he is equally confused who, while condemning any other system, social, political, or whatsoever, yet continues to act it out. Such a man does not, in his heart, regard the system as bad, but as good and just; this is evidenced by the fact that he continues to propagate it by his actions.

Systems are to men as light to the sun, rain to the clouds, or thoughts to the mind. They are both men and the deeds of men. To regard them as separate from men is confusion of thought and principle. Nor can there possibly be any injustice in their outworking, for the reaction of ignorant deeds is certain; the recompense of enlightened deeds is sure.

I see no evil in systems; I see evil in ignorance and wrong-doing. All systems are legitimate, for men have liberty to act in their own way. The ten gamblers who mutually agree to enrich and impoverish each other, have nobody to blame but themselves; and if the winners are satisfied with their gains, the losers should be equally satisfied with their losses; if they are not, then they should look to themselves and remedy their deeds. Their poverty is good discipline, in that it is driving them to seek a better way of action.

If a man regards a system as bad, he should withdraw from it in practice, and should bend his actions in another direction; for immediately two men act in concert, a system is formed, and the good and the bad which lurk in their actions will soon be manifested in the system which they have launched forth.

In the life of humanity, in systems, in what are called *good* and *bad*, is visible the outworking of the combined results of men's deeds; and in all, through all, and over all, justice reigns eternally triumphant.

Work, Wages and Well-Being

Activity is a necessity of existence, and usefulness is the object of being. Nature at once cuts off that which has become useless. Her economy is faultless, and she will not be burdened with things which have ceased to be of service in her progressive workshop. Nor does she allow her handy tools to lie unused, nor her bright things to rust. Wheresoever there is ability, there also are scope and opportunity; where there is energy, there also are legitimate channels for its exercise; where there is a soaring mind, the means of achievement are ready to hand. As the field waits for the plow, the sea for the ship, and the port for produce, so Nature in all her departments, whether material or mental, stands ready to cooperate with man in all his labors, and to reward him according to his diligence and industry. The statement "There is no scope for my abilities" is either an expression of vanity, an excuse for negligence, or a confession of lack of resource, or of inability to utilize opportunity. Ability need never lie unused for a moment. There is unlimited scope for all abilities. All that is required is the capacity for work.

Of all abilities, the capacity for work is the most useful and necessary, and its possession is a glorious power; and this men discover when they are disabled, or stricken down with sickness. When they are thus forcibly prevented from engaging in wholesome invigorating labor, what would they not give to have once again the spirited and glowing use of brain or muscle, or to spend exuberant strength in healthful exertion?

Work is of two kinds—it is either *loving labor* or *enforced slavery*. The man whose sole object is to get through his work in order to draw his pay, who has no love for, and no interest in, his work beyond what it represents in cash, is a slave and not a true worker. He labors only under the compulsion of necessity. His entire interest is in *getting* instead of in *doing*. He gives his labor irksomely and perfunctorily, but receives his pay with eagerness, striving, when he thinks he safely can, to give less and less labor, and get more and more wages. "Less work and more pay" is the cry of slaves and not of men.

On the contrary, the man whose heart is centered in his work, who aims at the perfect performance of his duty, is a true worker whose usefulness and influence are cumulative and progressive, carrying him on from success to greater and greater success, from low spheres of labor to higher and higher still. Thinking little or nothing of the wages, and much of the work; caring not for the gaining of reward, but eager and willing in service, he is sealed by Nature as one of her chosen sons, fitted by virtue of his unselfish labors to receive the greater excellence and the fuller reward.

For while full recompense may, and frequently does, escape the man who covetously seeks it, it cannot be withheld from him who ignores it in his work. For the true recompense is never withheld, but, in the selfish desire to secure the recompense without giving its equivalent, disappointment is the pay received, and the expected reward does not appear.

The wages of work are sure. In the universal economy no man is cheated; he cannot be defrauded of his just earnings, for every effort receives its proportionate result; first work as the cause, and then wages as the effect. But while wages is the result, it is not the end; it is only a means to a still greater and more far-reaching result and end, namely, the progress and increased happiness both of the individual and the race, in a word, to *well-being.*

The receiving of so much money for work done does not represent wages in its entirety; it is, indeed, only a small portion of the actual wages of true work; while the man who considers that the end of work is reached when he has received the money due, receives all he bargains for, he does not derive complete satisfaction from his labors, nor comprehend or enter the higher spheres of knowledge and usefulness, which are reserved for the devotees of unselfish duty.

It is a day of definitely marked progress in the life of a man when, by the illumination of spirit which proceeds from the development of a higher sense of duty, he passes from the burdensome sphere of slavery to the happy world of work; when he leaves behind him the grasping and bartering, the drudgery and humiliation, and, accepting his place among his fellows, becomes a cheerful cooperator with humanity, and a willing and happy instrument in the economy of things. Such a man receives the completion of wages in its sevenfold fullness as follows:

1. Money
2. Usefulness
3. Excellence
4. Power
5. Independence
6. Honor
7. Happiness

First, he receives the full amount of money of which his work is the equivalent; but in addition to this, his *usefulness* to the world is increased, and continues to increase in an ever-ascending degree; and this greater usefulness is one of the pure delights of labor, for one of the chief rewards of use is to be of greater use. To the slave, idleness is coveted as the reward of labor; but the worker rejoices in more work still.

This accumulating usefulness leads to the wages of *excellence*—skill, a growing perfection in the work undertaken; and every child that has learned its lesson, and every man and woman that has mastered a problem or a language, or surmounted a great difficulty, is acquainted with the happiness which is the sure accompaniment of such success; although, not until later do they realize the full significance of all that is involved in such success in relation to their career.

For a point of excellence is at last reached which merges into *power*—knowledge, mastery. The man who is devoted to his work, becomes at last a master in that work, whatever it may be. He becomes a teacher, a guide, and instructor to others who are treading the lower levels of the path up which he has climbed. He is sought out by others for the knowledge which he has acquired through practice and experience. He is relied upon, and takes his proper place among those who lead and serve mankind. Power is a form of wages received as the result of long and arduous labor. It is received only by him who has built it up, so to speak, who has earned it. The sowing of earnest and unselfish toil leads to the reaping of power.

Associated with power is *independence.* The true worker takes his place among his fellows as a useful citizen. The fearless flash of honesty is in his eyes, the ring of worth is in his voice, and the steadfastness of self-reliance is in his gait. He is not a drone in the human hive, but stands out in shining contrast to the skulking shirker who imagines that the highest good in life is to get something without working for it. The slave who goes to his hated work only because he is whipped to it by necessity, comes down to beggary and shame and is despised and neglected; but the true worker ascends into independence and honor, and is admired and sought.

Honor—this is one of the higher forms of wages, and it comes unerringly and unsought to all who are energetic and faithful in the work of their life. It may be, and often is, late in coming, but come it must and does, and always at its own proper time; for while money is the first and smallest item in wages, honor is one of the last and greatest; and the greater the honor, the longer and harder is the course of labor by which it is earned. There are degrees of honor according to the measure of usefulness, and the greatest men receive the greatest honor.

They who receive the fullness of wages, receive the fullness of *happiness*, for true work as surely brings about happiness, as idleness and enforced labor are paid in the coin of unhappiness. From the perfection of happiness proceeds well-being—a quiet conscience, a satisfied heart, a tranquil mind, and the consciousness of having increased the happiness, and aided in the progress of mankind through the full and faithful exercise of one's abilities.

First work, and then wages; but well-being only follows when the work is of the true kind, when it is loved for its own sake, and when the money received for such work is utilized for further work and better achievement instead of being squandered in folly and self-indulgence. Even he who only works for the pay in coin will derive just the measure of well-being which that pay can purchase if he spends it carefully, and will thus aid, in a small measure, industrial progress; but he can also, by a foolish use of his wages, make it an instrument of ill-being, and reduce himself to a dead and useless limb on the tree of life.

It is demanded by the law of things that every man shall receive the equivalent of what he gives. If he gives idleness he receives inactivity—death; if he gives stinted and unwilling service he receives stinted and hardly secured pay; if he gives loving and generous labor, he receives generous recompense in a life replete with blessedness.

It may here be asked, "But what about the toiling masses? What you say may be, and doubtless is, true of certain favored individuals, but how can it apply to the vast army of mill-workers and factory hands whose toil is long and hard and almost purely mechanical?"

It applies with equal force to them. There are no favored individuals; and there was a time when those who now occupy the high places stood in the low. There is no reason why the mill-worker should not be unselfish in his labor, and faithful and conscientious in duty; and there is every reason why he should economize his entire financial, physical and mental resources, using his money for the improvement of his home and surroundings and his evenings and spare time in the culture of his intellectual and moral powers. He will thus be preparing himself for higher spheres of usefulness and power, which will not be withheld from him when he is sufficiently equipped and strengthened to deal with intricate matters and carry weighty responsibilities; while the process of preparation itself will be one of ever-increasing knowledge, strength and happiness.

Work, wages and well-being are three broad stages in individual and racial evolution; and the political economy of the future will take into account those higher mental and spiritual forms of wages which it now ignores, but which are still the most powerful factors in the well-being of men and nations.

Well, indeed, will it be for that nation which is the first to realize and wisely utilize the fact that its prosperity and happiness are not limited to its material resources, but that in the mental and spiritual material of its inhabitants it possesses inexhaustible mines of living resources, which, when worked with the tools of suitably-evolved educational methods, will afford rich yields of prosperity and peace; that the surest and swiftest way to even material success—as well as to all the higher and nobler successes—is by the assiduous cultivation of character.

The Survival of the Fittest as a Divine Law

Nature and Spirit were at one time universally considered to be at enmity, and even today the majority of people regard them as opposed to each other; but a fuller knowledge of the Cosmos reveals the sublime fact that the natural and the spiritual are two aspects of One Eternal Truth.

Nature is the Spirit made visible and tangible. The seen is the expressed form and letter of the unseen. We search in trackless deserts of speculation to find the real, while all the time it stands before us. The return, from those weary and fruitless wanderings, to Truth is a coming back to the simple and obvious; but whereas we went out with sealed eyes, we come back with them unsealed: we look upon Nature with a vision clarified from ignorance and egotism, and lo! the unclean has become clean, the mortal has become immortal, the natural is seen to be also the spiritual.

Thus, when the physical scientist reveals a natural law, he, at the same time, makes known to the understanding mind—whether he himself knows it or not—a spiritual law. The whole universe is spiritual, and every physical law is the letter of a moral principle. When the moral nature of the Cosmos is apprehended, all controversies about matter and spirit—as things opposed—are at an end, and the assiduous worker in physical realms—often spoken of contemptuously as a "materialist"—is seen to be a *revealer*, as well as the worker in spiritual realms, the two phases of the universe being, as we have pointed out, but two arcs of one perfect whole.

When Charles Darwin made known the law of "the survival of the fittest," he revealed the working of Divine Justice in Nature. The almost universal prejudice and passionate opposition among religious people which the announcement of his discovery aroused was based, not on the fact itself, but upon a total misunderstanding of that law. That opposition has today nearly died out; but even yet one frequently hears this law referred to as a "cruel law," and the belief in it denounced as tending to destroy pity and love.

Such people always think of this law as "the survival of the cruelest," or "the survival of the strongest," and here is where the misunderstanding arises. The correct term, "The Survival of the *Fittest*," must not be lost sight of; for the fittest are never the cruelest, and rarely the strongest. The strongest and cruelest creatures have long since passed away, and have given place to weaker, but *more intelligent*, creatures and beings. Think of the numberless insects, and of the many powerful enemies which beset them on every hand. Yet these wonderful and beautiful creatures continue to flourish, and they owe their continuance to their intelligence, which is greater, better, and more fitted to survive than the strength and cruelty of their enemies. For what is the survival of the fittest but the survival of *the best?* In a world of continual progress, it must needs be that the best of every period takes precedence of the worst—the good of the bad, the fit of the unfit. This, indeed, is the very meaning of progress. When we think of progress, we at once think of something, by its superiority—its greater fitness to the time and occasion—taking precedence of something which is inferior and has fallen out of the line of advancement; and this progress, this advancement, this survival of the fittest, resolves itself into a moral principle, into a Divine Law.

Opponents of this teaching tacitly assume that the most selfish are the fittest to survive, and they thereupon condemn the teaching as callous, and accuse Darwin of making selfishness supreme. But the error is theirs, their's and not Darwin's or the law's. In their prejudice they wrest his meaning to a false issue, and attack that. Their error consists in assuming that the fittest to survive are the most selfish; whereas such are the worst specimens, and not the best. When we realize that the unselfish are more fitted to survive than the selfish, this law assumes an aspect the very opposite from that which its opponents have given it, and we at once see that in it are involved the profoundest moral principles, namely, the principles of Justice and Love.

Remembering that it is the *fittest* that survive, what, then—in this universe of law and order—constitutes the fittest? It is evident that the fittest are *the most advanced specimens of any given species*. Not the strongest, not the cruelest, not the most selfish, not even the finest physically; but *the most advanced*, those most in line with the order of evolution.

The fittest at one period are not the fittest at another. There was a time when brute force was dominant; but that was when nothing higher had been evolved. Yet even in that long distant period— ten million years back, when gigantic monsters held sway upon the earth—something higher was being evolved. Already, intelligence, yea, and unselfish love, were beginning to make themselves felt; for those great beasts loved and protected their young, and so all who most unselfishly shield their offspring, be they beasts or men, will be most protected, while, obviously, any species that neglected its offspring would rapidly perish.

Thus, long, long ages ago, the fragile babe of intelligence was born in the manger of brute force, and since then, through all the ages of struggle, it has been gradually but surely overcoming brutal strength and terror; so that today intelligence has conquered, or almost conquered; for the strongest brutes have passed away forever, having given place to beings physically weaker and smaller, but better and more morally perfect.

Without the operation of such a law man could never have come into existence; for man is, up to the present, the crown and summit of a process of struggle, selection, and progress which began many millions of years ago when the first of life appeared upon the earth. Man is the product of the law of the survival of the fittest operating through millions of years, perhaps millions of ages; yet in brute strength he is far inferior to many animals. He rules the earth today because of the principle of intelligence within him. But there is being evolved in man a higher principle and intelligence, namely, *Divine Love*, which is as much higher and more powerful than intelligence as intelligence is higher and more powerful than brute force. I use the term "*Divine Love*" in order to distinguish it from human affection and from that intermittent kindly impulse which are both spoken of as love. Intelligence may aid selfishness, but not so Love: in Love all selfishness is swallowed up and brute force is no more, both being transmuted into gentleness.

The beginnings of this Divine Love are already in the world. We see its wonderful operation in the few men in whom it has been perfected, namely, the Great Spiritual Teachers who, by their precepts and the example of their lives, rule the world today; and selfish men worship them as God. We see in these men the prophecy of what Love will do in the distant future, when a large number of men possess it in an advanced degree; how selfishness and selfish men will submit to it and be governed by it, as the brutes now submit to man's intelligence and are ruled by it. And this Love is making its appearance not only in the Great Teachers, but in men less evolved; and though in these it is, as yet, in a more or less rudimentary form, nevertheless, the stirrings of its gentleness and joy are being felt in many human hearts.

A common argument against the survival of the fittest is that were men to put it into practice, they would kill off all their weaklings and invalids, preserving only the strong, and thus destroying all pity and love and humanity. This argument is a demonstration of the error to which we have already referred. It is ludicrously self-contradictory; for, while it admits that the best elements are pity and love and humanity, it asserts that these would perish if the fittest, or best, survived. And here we are at the heart of the whole matter. *The best does survive*, and, therefore, pity, compassion, and love cannot be overthrown by selfishness and force, because they are superior qualities and will survive when selfishness is forever annihilated.

Speaking of human beings, it is plain that the fittest to survive are not the selfish and the cruel, but those who have developed the finest characteristics of kindness, compassion, justice, and love; in a word, the most moral, the purest, and wisest.

To talk about putting this law "into practice" shows ignorance of its nature; for it is independent in its operation, and is always in activity, and all men and creatures obey it; and should ever a race of men, under the mistaken notion that they were practicing it, do it such violence as to "kill off their weaklings and invalids," the law would not cease to operate in their case, and they, by virtue of that very law, would soon exterminate themselves.

With the ceaseless march of human progress, cruelty is becoming less and less fitted to survive against the growing intelligence and gentleness. The cruel races have nearly all died out, only disorganized remnants of them remaining. The fierce animals of prey are becoming fewer, and brutal men are now regarded as a menace to society. Gradually and inevitably, also, selfish and aggressive men will come to have less and less power in the world, will become more out of harmony with the growing environment of peace and good-will, till at last they will pass away from the earth altogether, as the gigantic brutes have passed away, no longer fitted to survive in a world conquered by Love, in which righteousness and truth become triumphant.

Thus this law, as represented by Darwin, is the aspect, in Nature, of the operation of Justice, or Love; for in the Light of Truth, Justice and Love are seen to be one. The spiritual aspect of the law was intimately known by all the Great Teachers, and men have overlooked the fact that these Teachers embodied it in their teaching. Thus the precept of Jesus, "The meek shall inherit the earth," is none other than a simple but Divine statement of the survival of the fittest.

Justice in Evil

Today we frequently meet with the assertion "All is good." Pope in his famous essay on man, said—

Whatever is, is right,

and nearly all are familiar with Browning's oft-quoted line—

God's in his heaven, all's right with the world.

In the face of these statements, the questions naturally arise: Are war and famine good? Are sickness and poverty good? Are sorrow and suffering good? These things belong to the category of the great facts of human life; are they good? Again, are sin and selfishness right? Are drunkenness and brutality right? Are crime and violence right? Are accidents by sea and land right? Are catastrophes involving hundreds of thousands of lives right? These things, like the former, are everyday facts. They are real, and cause wide-spread suffering; are they right?

Many persons must have questioned thus during the past years of unprecedented catastrophes in the form of volcanic eruptions, earthquakes, floods, famines, wars, and various forms of crimes and violence.

Are these things right? If so, why are men so eager to escape them? Even those who are given to quoting "Whatever is, is right" will, in the next breath, refer to certain "evils" and propose some method of being rid of them.

It is plain that in the sense of adding to human happiness, these things *are not right*, for they conduce to human misery. Even those who deny the existence of evil in theory recognize it in practice, in their efforts to conquer it.

Nevertheless, those statements as to the Universal Good and the rightness of all things, are true. It is all a matter of relativity. The recognition of evil, and the statement that all is good, are not contradictory. When the events of life are related to human happiness, then some are recognized as "good" and some as "evil," but when they are related to the fundamental and eternal principle of Justice, then all things are seen to be good, right, in harmony with the Great Law of inviolable Equity.

Take a simple example—that of physical pain. When we are considering human happiness, bodily pain is an evil, but when we consider the principle of Life itself, and its protection and continuance, then physical pain is seen to be good, as it is a warning monitor urging man to the protection of his body from hurt and extinction.

And it is with mental pain as with physical—with sorrow, remorse, loneliness and grief—it is evil because it destroys happiness; but as the effect of ignorance and wrong-doing it is just, and therefore good, as it urges men to seek the paths of wisdom and right-doing.

The prophet Isaiah says:

I form the light and create darkness; I make peace and create evil; I the Lord do all these things.

He thus recognizes the justice of evil, that it has its place in the moral universe as the opposite of good, just as darkness has its place in the physical universe as the opposite of light.

The prophet Amos expresses the same thing when he says:

> Shall there be evil in a city, and the Lord hath not
> done it?

The writings of the Hebrew prophets in the Old Testament teem with statements of the truth that evil is rooted in justice, not in injustice; that all the afflictions and calamities which overtake men spring from some violation, on man's part, of the moral law. So pronounced are they upon this point that they even attribute the suffering caused by purely external occurrences—such as floods, storms, earthquakes, drought, and dearth of food—to man's inward unrighteousness and his consequent departure from the Divine Order.

And, indeed, a profound acquaintance with the human heart and with human life does reveal the great truth—a truth never apparent on the surface, and therefore hidden from the shallow and unthinking—that all tragedy is the culminating point in the conflict of human passions. Where there are no violent passions there can be no tragedy, no disaster, no catastrophe. When humanity has attained to inward harmony and peace, it will be free from all those forms of violence which now devastate the world and scourge humankind with grief and lamentation.

Maeterlinck perceives this truth clearly, for in his *"Wisdom and Destiny,"* he says:

Fatality shrinks back abashed from the soul that has more than once conquered her; there are certain disasters she dare not send forth when this soul is near.

. . . The mere presence of the sage suffices to paralyze destiny; and of this we find proof in the fact that there exists scarce a drama wherein a true sage appears; when such is the case, the event must needs halt before reaching bloodshed and tears. Not only is there no drama wherein sage is in conflict with sage, but, indeed, there are very few whose action revolves round a sage. And, truly, can we imagine that an event shall turn into tragedy between men who have earnestly striven to gain knowledge of self ? . . . It is rarely indeed that tragic poets will allow a sage to appear on the scene, though it be for an instant. They are afraid of a lofty soul, for they know that events are no less afraid; and were there heroes to soar to the height the real hero would gain, their weapons would fall to the ground, and the drama itself become peace—the peace of enlightenment.

It is a significant fact that, while Shakespeare depicted nearly every type of character, he never brought a sage into his dramas. The truth is that his tragedies could not have taken place in the presence of a sage. Their outward violence stands related as *effect* to the hidden *cause* of disordered and conflicting passions. The sage has lifted himself above such disorder and conflict, and such is the power of his harmonious and tranquil spirit that, in his presence the passions of others will be calmed and subdued, and their approaching tragic issue averted.

It is a mighty truth, and one which stands clearly revealed in the mind of the sage and the prophet, that all the evils of humanity spring from the ignorance, and, therefore, from the mistakes, the wrongdoing of humanity itself. It is, therefore, just and right. But though just and right, it is not desirable; it is evil, and needs to be transcended. It is just and right, as imprisonment is just and right for the thief, in that it teaches man, and ultimately brings him to the feet of wisdom. As physical pain is a protector of man's body, so mental pain is a protector of his mind and of his life.

From man's ignorance of the Divine Law—of the Moral Order of the universe—arise those thoughts and passions—inward conditions—which are the source of tragedy, disaster, catastrophe. Envy, ill-will, jealousy, produce strife and quarreling, and ultimately bring about wars in which thousands are killed and disabled, and hundreds of homes are filled with mourning. Greediness, self-indulgence, and the thirst for pleasure lead through gluttony, indolence, and drunkenness to disease, poverty, and plague. Covetousness, lust and selfishness in all its forms cause men to practice deception, lying and dishonesty, and to strive against others in the blind pursuance of their petty plans and pleasures; thus leading to deprivation, loss and ruin; and where there are excessively violent passions there is always a violent life ending in a premature and violent death.

Man, by his ignorance, his selfishness, his darkness of mind, is the maker of sorrow, and the cause of catastrophe. His sufferings are indications that the Divine Law has been arrested, and is now asserting itself. The tragic darkness of his life is the outcome of that same Justice from which his joyful light proceeds. If every suicide, every ruin, every woe, even every accident, could be traced to its original cause in the moral constitution of things, its justice would be found to be without blemish.

And that which applies to individuals applies in the same way to nations. Widespread selfishness leads inevitably to widespread disaster; national corruption is followed by wholesale catastrophe, and by national disaster and ruin.

And not alone poverty, disease, and famine, but even earthquakes, volcanic eruptions, floods, and all such external happenings would be found, in their original cause, to be intimately related to men's moral life. That external accidents have a moral cause is plainly seen in the case of violent persons bringing about fatal accidents to themselves through folly and recklessness.

Man's body, both by chemical and gravitational affinity, is a portion of the earth, as his mind, both spiritually and ethically, is a portion of the Moral Order of the universe. His life and being are interwoven with, and are inseparable from, the very nature and constitution of things, and, being a moral entity, and therefore a reasonable agent, it is within the domain of his power to discover and work with the Divine Law instead of striving against it.

All man's pains, afflictions, disasters, calamities, are the shock resulting from running, either percipiently or blindly, against the Moral Law, as a reckless rider or blind man is hurt when he runs up against a wall; and these sorrows are not the arbitrary visitations and punishments of an offended Deity, but are matters of cause and effect, just as the pain of burning is the effect of coming into too close contact with fire.

In these days of social, political, and theological conflicts; and with wars, famines, floods, crimes, conflagrations, and volcanic and seismic catastrophes taking place on every hand, a return to the study of the Hebrew prophets—burning, as they are, with the fire of Truth on national matters and local catastrophes—would prove, not only scientifically enlightening, but would help considerably toward unveiling, in the mind of man, the revelation of the beauty and order of the Cosmos, and the perfect justice of human life.

The evils of life are right because of the causes which man has created; but man, having created causes which produce evil, can also create causes which produce good; and when the inward passions are tamed and subdued the outward violence will disappear, or will be powerless to hurt mankind.

Between the inward violence of surging passions and the outward violence of Nature there is such a close correspondence as to render them, in the inner order of things, of one indivisible essence. As the prophet Amos again puts it:

> For they know not to do right, saith the Lord, who store up violence and robbery in their palaces.

Therefore, thus saith the Lord God; an adversary there shall be round about the land; and he shall bring down thy strength from thee, and thy palaces shall be spoiled.

The outward "adversary" is necessary to nullify the inward violence, is brought into existence by it. When a nation becomes corrupt, it is conquered and swallowed up. When cities become morally bankrupt, they fall to pieces, or are destroyed by some outward force.

Justice and Love

One frequently hears justice referred to as being opposed to love. Such an error arises out of lack of understanding of the profound and comprehensive significance of these two principles; for two divine laws cannot stand in opposition or contradiction to each other. Two basic laws, both admittedly good, *must* harmonize, otherwise one would be evil, for good cannot oppose good. The antagonism which men place between justice and love does not exist in reality; it is an error arising from ignorance of the true nature and right application of the principles involved.

The element of kindness is never absent from justice; if it were, it would be cruelty and not justice. The element of severity is never absent from love; if it were, it would be weak emotionalism and not love. There is often more love in a severe reproof than in a yielding acquiescence. The father who has little love for his child, though he may not treat it cruelly, will not take pains to train it properly; but the father who has great love for his child will train it with a firm yet gentle hand. He will be just to his child because he loves it. He will administer correction and reproof when necessary, that his child may profit thereby.

Justice is not separate from love; love is not separate from justice. The essential oneness of the two principles is simply expressed in the divine edict—"Whatsoever a man soweth, that shall he also reap." It is in accordance both with perfect love and perfect justice that man should reap the good results of his good deeds, and the bad results of his bad deeds. All men admit this, theoretically, though the majority refuse to recognize the operation of such a law in the universe, arguing, when overtaken with trouble, that in their case they are not reaping what they have sown, as they have never done anything to call for such misfortune, but are suffering innocently (unjustly), or are afflicted through the wrong-doing of others.

Such a law, however, obtains, and those who will search long enough, and look deep below the surface of things, will find it and be able to trace, with precision, its faultless working. Nor would a right-minded man wish it to be otherwise. He would know that the kindest thing that could be done to him would be that he should suffer the full penalty of all his mistakes and wrong-doing, so that he might thereby grow more rapidly in virtue and wisdom. Petitions to Deity to abrogate the just punishment of sins committed are without avail, and can only spring from an immature moral sense. Woe indeed would descend upon man if the law of justice could thus be set aside.

Self-afflicted and torn with sorrow as he now is, there is hope in the law which bestows no special favors and is unfailingly just; but if man, by offering up a prayer could escape the effects of his bad deeds, then justice would be non-existent, and as for love, where would it be? For if one could thus be deprived of his *bad* earnings, what assurance could he have of not being robbed of his good earnings? Thus the ground of salvation would be cut away, and caprice and despotism would take the place of love and justice.

As a coin, which is one, has two distinct sides, so love and justice are two aspects of the same thing. Men do not perceive the love that is hidden in justice, nor the justice that is hidden in love, because they perceive only one side, and do not take pains to turn these principles round, as it were, and see them in their completion.

Justice, being a divine principle, cannot contain any element of cruelty. All its apparent harshness is the chastening fire of love. Man himself, and not the law per se, has brought about all the afflictions which are working for his ultimate happiness and good. Love reigns supreme in the universe because justice is supreme. A tender and loving hand administers the rod of chastisement. Man is protected even against himself. Love and justice are one.

Self-Protection: Animal, Human and Divine

Many and wonderful are the means and methods of self-protection in this world of combat! Natural history has revealed the fact that even plants employ means of self-protection; and when we come to the animal world, the methods adopted to avoid annihilation in the struggle for life are so numerous and remarkable as to call forth our admiration and wonder. Nor, in this fight for life is "the battle to the fierce and the race to the strong" in all cases. Indeed, the weak things of Nature exhibit such ingenuity in the means which they adopt to escape their enemies, that they are equally successful in holding their own with the fiercest creatures that have few enemies to fear. The insects, weakest of all creatures, have developed this self-protective ingenuity to a remarkable degree, even to imitating in color and form the twigs upon which they rest, adopting the hue of the soil or the dead or living leaves among which they live, and in some cases, through long experience, they have so closely imitated in color and form certain flowers which they habitually haunt that their enemies, the birds, keen as is their sight, pass them by; and even man, with all his intelligence, cannot distinguish them from the flowers unless he has had some experience as an observant naturalist. The smallest fishes adopt similar means of concealing themselves, although they are in the lowest class of animal life.

When we come to the quadrupeds, (although the weaker and smaller among them, those most hunted by the larger, adopt ruses similar to those which prevail among the insects and fishes) brute strength largely takes the place of stratagem. The beast has developed powerful weapons of defense, such as horns, fangs, claws, etc., combined with an iron or lithe muscularity, with which he maintains his place on the earth, and defies extinction. Endurance, speed, strength and ferocity are the means of self-protection among the brutes.

Animal self-protection reaches its highest excellence in the superb strength and cunning of the lion and the tiger, yet it appears weak and clumsy when compared with the means of self-protection adopted by man; for self-preservation, although it is not all-powerful in the human as in the animal world, is still a dominant impulse among human beings.

Man is possessed of the entire animal nature, and the animal impulses and instincts are strong within him, but there is, along with this animal life, an added intelligence and moral sense—a self-consciousness—by virtue of which his self-protective scope and power are greatly enlarged and intensified. He is still an animal, with endurance, speed, strength and ferocity, but he is also something more and greater—he is an intelligent, self-conscious being.

Among men of low order of intelligence, the animal methods still largely obtain. In the struggle of life, the savage relies on brute strength. Even among civilized communities, there are still thousands of admirers of "the noble art of self-defense," which can only be noble in the sense that we speak of the ferocity of the lion as being noble, and is devoid of art, being compounded entirely of brute force and cunning. Indeed, this practice is so closely allied to the beast that it has long ceased to be a means of self-defense among civilized men, and has become merely a vulgar pastime for the few.

Working along physical lines, and still following the well-worn track of animal instinct, man has invented numerous implements of destruction by which to annihilate his enemy and preserve himself, and upon these, with increasing ingenuity and subtlety, he continues to improve. Working along the new path of pure intelligence—which is pre-eminently the human, as distinguished from the animal sphere of activity—he discovers means of adding to his physical comforts and for the peaceful protection of his body, and asserts his right and power to live, not by brute force, but by toil of hand and keenness of brain. The basic struggle here, indeed, is not directly a fight for food and life, but for the artificial means by which food is procured and life maintained, namely, money. The fierce animal struggle has evolved into the more kindly human one; in place of the bloody strife with tooth and claw there is the more amicable combat of wit and skill. Man has discovered—though he has as yet only partially learned this—that there are better methods of self-protection than that of attacking, killing and despoiling others, that by such a method he endangers his own comfort, happiness, and even life, and that it is better to engage in a bloodless competition for supremacy and leave every person to take his place in life according to the measure of his mental capacity. Right has begun to take the place of might, and although the struggle is largely one for money, it is not altogether so, but is surely evolving into one for the securing of those mental qualities which increase man's nobility, and better fit him as an instrument of life and progress; such are the intellectual qualities of reason, judgment, tact, foresight, ingenuity, resource, inventiveness; and the moral qualities of kindness, forbearance, sympathy, forgiveness, reverence, honesty, justice. Human education at present is almost entirely along these intellectual and moral lines. The instruments by which man struggles with man for the capacity to live and to endure are faculties, not fangs; talents, not talons.

Intellectual and moral excellence constitute the passport to existence in the human world.

The intellectually vigorous and the morally upright take the lead in the race of life. Nevertheless, the weaker ones take their place, and have scope and opportunity for development. Slowly man is learning that in the protection of others—the weak, the suffering and the afflicted—he is affording a surer protection for himself.

In such methods of self-protection we perceive an enormous advance upon the savage instinct of the brute. Commerce, crafts, and games take the place of plunder and destruction; and limited animal affection is enlarged to benevolence and philanthropy. In human competition the brute still lurks, but its ferocity is subdued, its nature is largely transmuted into something better, more beneficent; its dark horror is lightened up with the warm rays of kindness; its harshness is softened by the gentleness of a larger and ever-increasing love.

But high as is human over animal self-protection, there is another form of self-protection that is as high above the human as that is above the animal, and that is divine, or spiritual protection. By this method the man does not fight with others physically, after the manner of the brute, he does not struggle with others mentally, as does the human being; he fights with the brute within himself, in order to annihilate it; he struggles with the greed in his own nature, that he may fit himself to live the higher, nobler, more enduring life of peace, good-will and wisdom.

In divine protection, the fierce struggle with others is at an end, the competition of self-interest is no more, and the weapons employed are self-sacrifice and non-resistance. And these weapons can only be understood and employed by him whose moral elevation is such as to gain him admittance to the World of Divine Things. Just as the fanged and taloned brute cannot grasp and use those mental weapons of resource and inventiveness which the more highly endowed and talented human being employs with such ease and power, so the self-seeking man cannot comprehend and wield those instruments of self-sacrifice and non-resistance with which the divine man not merely shields himself, but protects the whole world.

Self-interest, resistance to, and competition with others are the most powerful factors in the purely human life, but in the divine life, self-obliteration and deep-felt sympathy with and compassion for others are the dominant motives.

The divine man conquers by non-retaliation, and by yielding where others enter into selfish strife; and his gentle powers are so invincible that the lesser selfish powers, great and potent as those are when compared with the merely animal equipments, dissolve away in ineffectual weakness. As bestial instincts cannot vie with human powers, so human powers cannot stand against divine principles, and the divine man stands upon, and acts upon, such principles. In him the human qualities mentioned are merged into the divine principles of Patience, Humility, Purity, Compassion and Love.

Both the animal and the human are concerned only with the protection and preservation of the body which is temporal, but the divine man's preservation is concerned with the spirit which is eternal, like the principles upon which he stands. In a word, divine preservation consists in preserving the mind from passion and selfishness, and imbuing it with pureness and wisdom.

We get a glimpse into the vast power inherent in self-sacrifice and non-resistance when we contemplate the lives and characters of the few divine men who practiced these principles—in Jesus, Buddha, and others. All men, broadly speaking, yield and bow down to these great Masters in Divine Things. Men who have reached the greatest heights in worldly achievement—monarchs, conquerors, successful generals, statesmen, orators, financiers—bow in humble reverence and awe before the names of those Great Ones, recognizing intuitively that their own conquests and achievements, with all their worldly glory, are as nothing compared with that supreme self-conquest, that mighty spiritual achievement which those gentle teachers of mankind exhibited. Today some five hundred millions of people bow down to Buddha as their Guide and Master, and some three hundred millions likewise bend before Jesus as their Savior and the Keeper of their lives.

In these three methods of self-protection—animal, human, and spiritual—we perceive the fundamental forces which are at work in the evolution of sentient beings; an evolution beginning with the lowest creature and extending to the divinest being of whom we have any direct knowledge. We also see that there is no inherent evil in any of these methods, that all are equally legitimate, and belong to the cosmic order of things. Each in its own sphere is right and necessary, leading to higher and higher intelligence, and deeper and deeper knowledge. The animal defends itself in accordance with its nature and the limits of its knowledge; the human being protects itself likewise in harmony with the dictates of his human nature; and the divine being eternally preserves himself in peace and blessedness by virtue of his clearer insight and deeper wisdom.

Nor is any measure of force lost during the process of evolution. The brute passion is, in man, transmuted into intellectual and moral energy, and in the divine man both are merged into control and equanimity.

Aviation
and the New
Consciousness

D r. Bucke in his work, *"Cosmic Consciousness,"* published some ten years ago, stated that aerial navigation would become an accomplished fact in the near future, and that it would revolutionize the social and economic conditions of the world.

So far as the advent of the new means of travel is concerned, he has proved to be a true prophet, and I am convinced that his prophecy of its revolutionizing aspect will shortly begin to be proved true. Of this great revolution in its completion Dr. Bucke says:

Before aerial navigation boundaries, tariffs, and, perhaps, distinctions of language will fade out. Great cities will no longer have reason for being and will melt away. The men who now dwell in cities will inhabit in summer the mountains and the seashores; building often in airy and beautiful spots, now almost or quite inaccessible, commanding the most extensive and magnificent views. In the winter they will probably dwell in communities of moderate size. As the herding together, as now, in great cities, so the isolation of the worker of the soil will become a thing of the past. Space will be practically annihilated, there will be no crowding together and no enforced solitude.

The above is a beautiful picture of the result upon human society, of the discovery of aviation, and it will no doubt prove true. Not that such a condition will be brought about rapidly. It will at least require several hundred years, and it is highly probable that it will be several thousand years before it is fully realized. As yet we are only in the crudest beginnings of flying, and the mastery of the air as a medium of human transit affords more scope for improvement and invention than any of the mechanical modes of locomotion hitherto employed. Invention will follow upon invention, through a long period of time, until men will be able to propel themselves through the air with a swiftness, a safety, and a skill perhaps equal to that of the migratory birds of the swiftest type. It was Edison who long years ago declared that the ultimate and perfected flying-machine would be built on the principle of the bird. While conforming more or less to this principle, the present machines are more on the principle of the kite, the motor-driving power taking the place of the string. In his book, "*The Coming Race*," Lord Lytton describes the individuals of that race as each possessing a pair of mechanical wings which were under the complete control of the operator, and by means of which he soared into the air and propelled himself gracefully through space. Doubtless this will be the form which the perfected flying-machine will take, and it conforms to that "principle of the bird" referred to by Edison.

But the phase of aviation with which we are here concerned is that which connects it with the evolving consciousness of man; for out of that self-consciousness, which is now man's dominant condition, and which is inevitably connected with struggle and suffering, with labor and sorrow, the beginnings of a higher, diviner form of consciousness are making their appearances. From man's present state of imperfection, combined with ceaseless aspiration toward a better, but as yet undefined, state, there is surely coming, as from a matrix, a new order of life, a more blessed condition, a greatly evolved form of consciousness hitherto unknown to man except in a few isolated cases.

Invention is allied to progress, is, indeed, an outward manifestation of inward growth. All man's inventions are adaptations to his expanding consciousness, and they definitely mark important turning points in the evolution of the race. At the moment of man's necessity, the new and needed thing appears. Just as the human intellect was preparing to break from the bonds of old superstitions, and sally forth in joyous and untrammeled freedom, the printing press appeared as the chief instrument of man's liberation. The coming of the steam engine tallied with the accelerated speed of human thought as it began to shake off its ancient lethargy; and when the expanding human mind could no longer move in a contracted local circle, or remain satisfied with petty selfish differences, the locomotive came forth to meet man's wider range, and to afford him scope for his increased mental activities and enlarged sympathies.

And now another invention has entered the field of actuality; one growing out of, yet more important than, any which have preceded it—that of flying. Man has hitherto employed the solid earth and the less solid water as the medium of material transit, but now he is to make an obedient servant of the tenuous atmosphere, using it to speed, bird-like, directly to his desired destination. And this is an important outward sign of the new stride in evolution which the race is now taking. Rapid and restless changes are marking the present transition period. Old religions and forms of government are passing away. New modes of thought and action are everywhere appearing. Man's consciousness is expanding. The *human* form of consciousness is about to touch, is indeed touching, the point of completion, and from it there will spring, is already springing, the *Divine* form of consciousness which is destined to transform the entire human race. For under that reign of consciousness, nearly everything, as it at present obtains in the world, will be reversed. Man, being then Divine, will act divinely. All those powerful human passions which now dominate the race, and are the chief springs of action will then take a subordinate place, and will be under the control and guidance of man's Divine will and wisdom. He will be master of himself and master of the earth.

Already man has been feeling the growing wings of this new consciousness wherewith he will soar into the highest regions of knowledge and blessedness. For ages, and under the guise of numerous religions, he has aspired to it, and the prophets have foretold it, and now he is to obtain his Divine birthright.

Aviation is the first outward symbol, as it were, of this new mind which is now taking shape. It is also more than a symbol, for it will form the first important material instrument by the aid of which the new consciousness will begin to materialize its glorious ideas and magnificent schemes for the happiness of the race, for the so-called happiness of today is misery compared with that blessed state which will obtain on the earth when the Divine condition has become well established.

The beginnings of this new condition, as aided by aviation, will be noticed in the breaking down of certain material limitations between man and man and between nations, and the disappearance of war; along with it will come a free and fraternal industrial intercourse between the nations, and a growing tendency to adopt in practice those fundamental religious principles which are universal, and thus to inaugurate one great world-wide religion. As aviation becomes more perfected, and enters into man's economical schemes, these new conditions—the first seedlings, as it were, of the new consciousness—will begin to appear, for when men are rapidly flitting from country to country, from continent to continent, on "the wings of the wind" they will be brought so close together, both socially and industrially, that the old animosities, which now exist between them, will die out, the old national barriers will quietly break down and disappear, and, without any revolutionary upheaval, the nations will become as one country, sinking all those interests which are not for the mutual good of all nations.

The locomotive is an instance of the above, though in the region of self-consciousness, in that it rendered civil war impossible, making of each nation, formerly divided against itself, a united family working harmoniously together. Aviation, however, will be connected with a higher region of consciousness altogether, namely, the cosmic consciousness, and its results will be much more striking and more far-reaching than those which have hitherto taken place in man's self-conscious condition.

At present we are only in the experimental stage of aviation, but this will be quickly followed by the economic stage, in which flying will be adapted to human travel and mercantile uses, and almost immediately this is reached the new conditions in societies and nations will begin to manifest themselves, and once having commenced, they will gradually absorb the old forms of life, using them as material on which to feed their growing beauty and grandeur. And new and grand men will arise having this higher consciousness, and they will be the leading instruments in establishing this new order of things upon the earth.

The New Courage

The virtue of courage is generally referred to in its physical manifestation, and it is significant in this particular—that its symbol is a beast of prey, namely, the lion. The dictionary rendering adheres to this physical aspect of courage, for on turning up the word I find its meanings are given as "bravery, fearlessness, intrepidity"; no other rendering being given. The soldier is the human type of courage, and the current sayings concerning courage are: "As courageous as a lion" and "As brave as a soldier."

The lion and the soldier are alike fearless in attack and defense, and both will forfeit life rather than yield; but it is an entirely animal physical attack and defense. Courage, however, cannot be Confined to this phase—indeed, this is its lowest manifestation,—for it has many aspects, many modes of action, and as man rises in the moral and spiritual scale, his courage becomes transmuted, taking a newer and higher form; but before proceeding to the highest form of courage, which is the subject of this article, it is necessary that the lower forms should be first considered.

With the physical form of courage already referred to all are familiar. It is common both to animals and men. It arises in fearlessness. Its twofold mode of action is *attack and defense.* It will be seen, however, that this kind of courage is inevitably associated with suffering, even with destruction and death, as daily manifested both in the animal and human spheres of life; self-protection being its dominant motive, whether in attack or defense.

But man is not only and merely an animal, a physical being; he is also a moral and intellectual being; and along with his moral evolution he began to develop a higher kind of courage—not the highest or the *New Courage* herein referred to; but yet a great advance on the purely animal courage— namely, *moral courage.* In physical courage the other person's body or property is attacked, while one's own body or property is defended. In moral courage the other person's ideas, opinions, or principles are attacked, one's own ideas, opinions, and principles being defended. There is the same fearlessness, the same attack and defense so far as the spirit of courage is concerned, but as regards its letter, these conditions have undergone a change; their physical aspect has disappeared, and, having undergone a process of transmutation, has reappeared in a new form, for moral courage is concerned, not with persons as persons, but with their principles; it is, indeed, purely mental, and while it is still concerned with destruction and is associated with suffering, the destruction is a bloodless and intellectual one, namely, the destruction of other men's opinions, and its suffering is mental and not physical.

This form of courage is now generally recognized, and is always referred to as moral courage, to distinguish it from common or physical courage. It is, without doubt, a comparatively recent development in the evolution of the race, and is entirely absent from animals. A few thousand years ago it was, in all probability, an exceeding rare and new faculty, and it is still in process of development, large numbers of the race not yet having evolved it; for while it is probable that at least seventy-five per cent of the race possess a considerable development of physical courage, it is doubtful whether twenty per cent possess any marked degree of moral courage; so much so that those in full possession of it are marked off from their fellows as men of a higher grade of character, and generally—though not necessarily and always—as leaders of men in their particular sphere of action.

But the New Courage, up to a consideration of which the preceding remarks have been leading, is a still higher form of courage; is, indeed, as much above and beyond moral courage as moral courage is above and beyond physical courage; and is as separate and distinct from it as that is from its precedent form. I have called it the New Courage because it is now new in the race; its manifestation being at present very rare, and, therefore, little understood. Though very different from moral courage, it results from it, just as moral courage though very different from physical courage results from it. Physical courage is of the animal; moral courage is of the human; the New Courage is of the Divine. The New Courage is, therefore, Divine fearlessness as distinguished from animal or human fearlessness.

This Divine fearlessness has a two-fold aspect. It at first consists in fearlessly attacking and overcoming the enemies within one's own mind—instead of the enemies without, as in the other two forms of courage—and is afterwards characterized by an entirely new method of conduct toward others, especially where external enmity and opposition have to be met. It is its latter and perfected stage with which we are here concerned—that is, with its outward manifestation.

We have seen how a man having physical courage acts in defense of his life and property; also how a man having moral courage acts in defense of his opinions; and now, how does one act who has Divine courage?

He who has the New Courage does not attack other men or defend himself; does not attack their opinions or defend his own; he is the defender of all men, and that from which he defends them is their own folly, their own ungoverned passions. While never seeking to protect himself, he so acts as to shield others from their deadliest enemy, namely, the evil within themselves.

Both physical and moral courage make much noise. In the one there is the clash of arms and the roar of artillery, along with the shouts of the victorious and the groans of the dying; in the other, there is the fierce war of opinions and the clamor of conflicting tongues. But in the New Courage there is a profound silence; yet this silence has more influence and enduring power in *one man* than that noise has in entire humanity. The New Courage may, indeed, be described as *the courage*

to be silent. Thus, when the man of Divine courage is attacked, abused, or slandered, he remains
serenely silent. Yet this is not a proud and selfish
silence. It is a silence based upon a right knowledge
of life, and having a profound and beneficent purpose; that purpose being the good of the attacking
person (and, through him, of all mankind) by protecting him from the evil passion by which he is so
injuriously influenced.

To remain silent, calm, and compassionate
in the midst of a seething sea of human passions externally pressing upon one—to achieve
this requires a lofty courage such as is yet almost
unknown to men; so much so that the few men
who have it, although misunderstood and perse-
cuted through life, are afterwards worshiped by
mankind as Divine and miraculous beings. And
here we see how this courage continues to operate
even after its possessor is gone from mortal vision.
The physically courageous man conquers another
in fight; the morally courageous man conquers the
opinions of many men, and wins thousands to his
cause; but the divinely courageous man conquers
the world, and his conquest is one of blessedness
and peace, and not of bloodshed or party strife.

In the New Courage, attack and defense, as they
obtain in the two lower kinds of courage, have
entirely disappeared; nevertheless, they have not

been destroyed; they still exist in the spirit, but have become blended into one, have been transmuted into a sublime and universal *kindness*; for when the Divine man refrains from engaging in combat with his adversary, and lets him go feeling that he has all the victory, it is because his thought is all for his mistaken enemy, and not for his own defense. He is prompted by a profound compassion for his enemy, a compassion based on Divine and perfect knowledge; and if his silent act does not always subdue the passions of his adversary at the time being, it subdues the passions of thousands of men through hundreds of future generations, merely by its recital; so great and far-reaching is the power of one deed of truth.

In the New Courage, then, silent kindness (and by this is meant something vastly different from that human impulse commonly called kindness) is both attack and defense. Instead of attempting to conquer passion by fiercer passion—which is the human way—it conquers it, and far more successfully, by its opposite, namely, *gentleness*, which is the Divine way. In the human sense, passion is not opposed at all, but is left alone; yet, in reality, it is opposed by something far more powerful than passion, for in all combats between Divine gentleness and human passion gentleness is the supreme victor. Thus, the man of Divine courage, while viewed from the lower standards of bravery, is not protecting or defending himself, and may for the time being be regarded as a coward, is, in reality, defending himself far more perfectly and successfully than the passionate fighters and partisans; for he who protects his enemy with love, and shields all men with the acts of Divine gentleness, is throwing around himself an eternal shield and protection.

For instances of this New Courage one has to go to the Great Spiritual Leaders of the race, so rare is it. The most striking instance is that of Jesus, who, when mocked, smitten, and crucified, did not retaliate, or offer the least resistance, or speak a word in self-defense; and the fact that the rabble taunted Him with the accusation "He saved others, Himself He cannot save" seems to show that they regarded Him both as an impostor and a coward. Think of the sublime courage required to pass through such an ordeal, and you will have some conception as to how far the New Courage transcends the ordinary human forms of bravery. That transcendent act of courage, too, is today universally recognized as Divine, and it still continues to lift men above their warring, selfish passions.

When the Buddha was abused and falsely accused by his enemies He always remained silent, and it not infrequently happened that those who came as accusing enemies went away as worshiping friends and disciples, so powerful was His silent gentleness.

It will be long, as we count time, before such courage becomes general in the race; but everything is making toward it. Other men will come who possess it, and then more and more, until at last the race will stand at this Divine level; then selfishness and sorrow will be ended, and the painful conflict of human passions will no more be heard upon earth.

James Allen:
A Memoir

By Lily L. Allen

from *The Epoch* (February–March 1912)

> *Unto pure devotion*
> *Devote thyself: with perfect meditation*
> *Comes perfect act, and the right-hearted rise—*
> *More certainly because they seek no gain—*
> *Forth from the bands of body, step by step.*
> *To highest seats of bliss.*

James Allen was born in Leicester, England, on November 28th, 1864. His father, at one time a very prosperous manufacturer, was especially fond of "Jim," and before great financial failures overtook him, he would often look at the delicate, refined boy, poring over his books, and would say, "My boy, I'll make a scholar of you."

The Father was a high type of man intellectually, and a great reader, so could appreciate the evident thirst for education and knowledge which he observed in his quiet studious boy.

As a young child he was very delicate and nervous, often suffering untold agony during his school days through the misunderstanding harshness of some of his school teachers, and others with whom he was forced to associate, though he retained always the tenderest memories of others—one or two of his teachers in particular, who no doubt are still living.

He loved to get alone with his books, and many a time he has drawn a vivid picture for me, of the hours he spent with his precious books in his favourite corner by the home fire; his father, whom he dearly loved, in his arm chair opposite also deeply engrossed in his favourite authors. On such evenings he would question his father on some of the profound thoughts that surged through his soul—thoughts he could scarcely form into words—and the father, unable to answer, would gaze at him long over his spectacles, and at last say: "My boy, my boy, you have lived before"—and when the boy eagerly but reverently would suggest an answer to his own question, the father would grow silent and thoughtful, as though he *sensed* the future man and his mission, as he looked at the boy and listened to his words—and many a time he was heard to remark, "Such knowledge comes not in one short life."

There were times when the boy startled those about him into a deep concern for his health, and they would beg him not to *think so much*, and in after years he often smiled when he recalled how his father would say—"Jim, we will have you in the Churchyard soon, if you think so much."

Not that he was by any means unlike other boys where games were concerned. He could play leap-frog and marbles with the best of them, and those who knew him as a man—those who were privileged to meet him at "Bryngoleu"—will remember how he could enter into a game with all his heart. Badminton he delighted in during the summer evenings, or whenever he felt he could.

About three years after our marriage, when our little Nora was about eighteen months old, and he about thirty-three, I realized a great change coming over him, and knew that he was renouncing everything that most men hold dear that he might find Truth, and lead the weary sin-stricken world to Peace. He at that time commenced the practice of rising early in the morning, at times long before daylight, that he might go out on the hills—like One of old—to commune with God, and meditate on Divine things. I do not claim to have understood him fully in those days. The light in which he lived and moved was far too white for my earth-bound eyes to see, and a *sense of it only* was beginning to dawn upon me. But I knew I dare not stay him or hold him back, though at times my woman's heart cried out to do so, waiting him all my own, and not then understanding his divine mission.

Then came his first book, "From Poverty to Power." This book is considered by many his best book. It has passed into many editions, and tens of thousands have been sold all over the world, both authorized and pirated editions, for perhaps no author's works have been more pirated than those of James Allen.

As a private secretary he worked from 9 a.m. to 6 p.m., and used every moment out of office writing his books. Soon after the publication of "From Poverty to Power" came "All These Things Added," and then "As a Man Thinketh," a book perhaps better known and more widely read than any other from his pen.

About this time, too, the "Light of Reason" was founded and he gave up all his time to the work of editing the Magazine, at the same time carrying on a voluminous correspondence with searchers after Truth all over the world. And ever as the years went by he kept straight on, and never once looked back or swerved from the path of holiness. Oh, it was a blessed thing indeed to be the chosen one to walk by the side of his earthly body, and to watch the glory dawning upon him!

He took a keen interest in many scientific subjects, and always eagerly read the latest discovery in astronomy, and he delighted in geology and botany. Among his favourite books I find Shakespeare, Milton, Emerson, Browning, The Bhagavad-Gita, the Tao-Tea-King of Lao-Tze, the Light of Asia, the Gospel of Buddha, Walt Whitman, Dr. Bucke's Cosmic Consciousness, and the Holy Bible.

He might have written on a wide range of subjects had he chosen to do so, and was often asked for articles on many questions outside his particular work, but he refused to comply, consecrating his whole thought and effort to preach the Gospel of Peace.

When physical suffering overtook him he never once complained, but grandly and patiently bore his pain, hiding it from those around him, and only we who knew and loved him so well, and his kind, tender Doctor, knew how greatly he suffered. And yet he stayed not; still he rose before the dawn to meditate, and commune with God; still he sat at his desk and wrote those words of Light and Life which will ring down through the ages, calling men and women from their sins and sorrows to peace and rest.

Always strong in his complete manhood, though small of stature physically, and as gentle as he was strong, no one ever heard an angry word from those kind lips. Those who served him adored him; those who had business dealings with him trusted and honoured him. Ah! how much my heart prompts me to write of his self-sacrificing life, his tender words, his gentle deeds, his knowledge and his wisdom. But why? Surely there is no need, for do not his books speak in words written by his own hand, and will they not speak to generations yet to come?

About Christmas time I saw the change coming, and understood it not—blind! blind! blind! I could not think it possible that *he* should be taken and *I* left.

But we three—as if we knew—clung closer to each other, and loved one another with a greater love—if that were possible—than ever before. Look at his portrait given with the January "Epoch," and reproduced again in this, and you will see that even then our Beloved, our Teacher and Guide, was letting go his hold on the physical. He was leaving us then, and we didn't know it. Often I had urged him to stop work awhile and rest, but he always gave me the same answer, "My darling, when I stop I must go, don't try to stay my hand."

And so he worked on, until that day, Friday, January 12, 1912, when, about one o'clock he sat down in his chair, and looking at me with a great compassion and yearning in those blessed eyes, he cried out, as he stretched out his arms to me, *"Oh, I have finished, I have finished, I can go no further, I have done."*

Need I say that everything that human aid and human skill could do was done to keep him still with us. Of those last few days I dare scarcely write. How could my pen describe them? And when we knew the end was near, with his dear hands upon my head in blessing, he gave his work and his beloved people into my hands, charging me to bless and help them, until I received the call to give up my stewardship!

"I will help you," he said, "and if I can I shall come to you and be with you often."

Words, blessed words of love and comfort, *for my heart alone* often came from his lips, and a sweet smile ever came over the pale calm face when our little Nora came to kiss him and speak loving words to him, while always the gentle voice breathed the tender words to her—*"My little darling!"*

So calmly, peacefully, quietly, he passed from us at the dawn on Wednesday, January 24, 1912. "Passed from us," did I say? Nay, only the outer garment has passed from our mortal vision. He lives! and when the great grief that tears our hearts at the separation is calmed and stilled, I think that we shall know that he is still with us. We shall again rejoice in his companionship and presence.

When his voice was growing faint and low, I heard him whispering, and leaning down to catch the words I heard—"At last, at last—at home— my wanderings are over"—and then, I heard no more, for my heart was breaking within me, and I felt, for *him* indeed it was "*Home at last!*" but for me—And then, as though he knew my thoughts, he turned and again holding out his hands to me, he said: "I have only one thing more to say to you, my beloved, and that is I love you, and I will be waiting for you; good-bye."

I write this memoir for those who love him, for those who will read it with tender loving hearts, and tearful eyes; for those who will not look critically at the way in which I have tried to tell out of my lonely heart this short story of his life and passing away—for *his* pupils, and, therefore, my friends.

We clothed the mortal remains in *pure white linen*, symbol of his fair, pure life, and so, clasping the photo of the one he loved best upon his bosom—they committed all that remained to the funeral pyre.

About the Author

James Allen was one of the pioneering figures of the self-help movement and modern inspirational thought. A philosophical writer and poet, he is best known for his book *As a Man Thinketh*. Writing about complex subjects such as faith, destiny, love, patience, and religion, he had the unique ability to explain them in a way that is simple and easy to comprehend. He often wrote about cause and effect, as well as overcoming sadness, sorrow and grief.

Allen was born in 1864 in Leicester, England into a working-class family. His father travelled alone to America to find work, but was murdered within days of arriving. With the family now facing economic disaster, Allen, at age 15, was forced to leave school and find work to support them.

During stints as a private secretary and stationer, he found that he could showcase his spiritual and social interests in journalism by writing for the magazine *The Herald of the Golden Age*.

In 1901, when he was 37, Allen published his first book, *From Poverty to Power*. In 1902 he began to publish his own spiritual magazine, *The Light of Reason* (which would be retitled *The Epoch* after his death). Each issue contained announcements, an editorial written by Allen on a different subject each month, and many articles, poems, and quotes written by popular authors of the day and even local, unheard of authors.

His third and most famous book *As a Man Thinketh* was published in 1903. The book's minor popularity enabled him to quit his secretarial work and pursue his writing and editing career full time. He wrote 19 books in all, publishing at least one per year while continuing to publish his magazine, until his death. Allen wrote when he had a message—one that he had lived out in his own life and knew that it was good.

In 1905, Allen organized his magazine subscribers into groups (called "The Brotherhood") that would meet regularly and reported on their meetings each month in the magazine. Allen and his wife, Lily Louisa Oram, whom he had married in 1895, would often travel to these group meetings to give speeches and read articles. Some of Allen's favorite writings, and those he quoted often, include the works of Shakespeare, Milton, Emerson, the Bible, Buddha, Whitman, Trine, and Lao-Tze.

Allen died in 1912 at the age of 47. Following his death, Lily, with the help of their daughter, Nora took over the editing of *The Light of Reason*, now under the name *The Epoch*. Lily continued to publish the magazine until her failing eyesight prevented her from doing so. Lily's life was devoted to spreading the works of her husband until her death at age 84.

CPSIA information can be obtained
at www.ICGtesting.com
Printed in the USA
LVHW080210240719
625115LV00007B/137/P